12-01

FISHING BOATS

BOATS & SHIPS

Jason Cooper

The Rourke Corporation, Inc.
Vero Beach, Florida 32964

PHOTO CREDITS:
© Francis Caldwell/Affordable Photo Stock: pages 10, 15; courtesy Grady-White Boats, Inc.: pages 13, 18; courtesy Regulator Marine, Inc.: page 4; © Lynn M. Stone: cover, title page, page 7, 8, 12, 17; courtesy Tracker Marine: page 21

CREATIVE SERVICES:
East Coast Studios, Merritt Island, Florida

EDITORIAL SERVICES:
Susan Albury

Library of Congress Cataloging-in-Publication Data

Cooper, Jason, 1942-
    Fishing boats / by Jason Cooper.
        p. cm. — (Boats)
    Includes bibliographical references and index.
    Summary: Surveys the uses, parts, and different kinds of fishing boats.
    ISBN 0-86593-562-9
    1. Fishing boats—Juvenile literature.
[1. Fishing boats.]
I. Title II. Series: Cooper, Jason, 1942- Boats & ships
SH344.8.B6C66   1999
623.8' 28—dc21   99–15115
                                                         CIP

Printed in the USA

TABLE OF CONTENTS

FISHING BOATS

Is there any better reason for having a boat than to fish? Not if you're a fisherman—or woman.

You can fish from almost any boat if its **deck** (DEK) isn't too far above the water. It would be tough to fish from the deck of an ocean liner. But some boats are made just for fishermen. They have the special features fishermen want.

Some fishing boats are **multipurpose** (MUL tuh pur pus) boats. They may be useful for fishing and other types of water activities, like skiing.

Fishing boats used for sport are quite a bit different from those used for **commercial** (kuh MUR shuhl) fishing.

The thrill of fighting a fish makes sportfishing a favorite American sport. Sportfishing boats bring fishermen and women to the fish.

COMMERCIAL FISHING BOATS

Commercial fishermen catch fish for a living. Their job is the commerce, or sale, of fish. They sell their catch to restaurants, markets, and **canneries** (KAN nur reez). Canneries seal up cans of fish, such as tuna and salmon.

The commercial fishing boats are quite large. Most of them work on the oceans. The smallest commercial fishing boats are about 25 feet (8 meters) long. The largest reach about 260 feet (80 meters), and they are more accurately called ships rather than boats.

Heavy with the day's catch, a commercial fishing boat returns to port in Homer, Alaska.

KINDS OF COMMERCIAL FISHING BOATS

Boats that fish fairly close to sea coasts range from about 25 feet (8 meters) to 130 feet (40 meters) in length. As you can tell, there is a great variety of coastal boats. A few have one- or two-person crews. Others may have 20 or more workers aboard.

Coastal boats may fish for a day and return to port. Or they may spend several days at sea.

The Pacific Sun, *a coastal fishing boat, rests in sunlight at the harbor in Seldovia, Alaska.*

The largest commercial boats can stay at sea for months. This type of **vessel** (VEH sul) includes ships that are built to catch, **process** (PRAH sess), and freeze fish.

These ships may have crews of 100 men and women. They can catch, process, and freeze over 80 tons (72,575 kilograms) of fish per day!

Both Russia and the United States have several of these catch-and-process ships.

Long-liners haul black cod aboard on the fishing vessel Martin *in the Gulf of Alaska.*

A lobster trap lies on the rear deck of the Frances Inez *in Southwest Harbor, Maine. Rugged lobster fishing boats chug out to sea and drop traps nearly every day.*

A woman operates this V-hull sportfishing boat from the console controls. The fishermen have plenty of room to fish along the sides of the deck.

COMMERCIAL FISHING

Many of the commercial boats are named for the method they use to fish. A seiner, for example, is a boat or ship that fishes with a **seine** (SANE) net.

Seiners catch more than half of the fish American ships take from the ocean. Most seines are purse-shaped. They're dragged by the ship near the ocean surface. Some are over one mile (1.6 kilometers) long.

A trawler drops a net called a **trawl** (TROL). A trawl is a funnel-shaped net used in water up to 3,300 feet (1,000 meters) deep.

The salmon seiner Paragon *sets her net in the Baranoff Islands of Alaska.*

A long-liner fishes with a long fishing line. As many as 2,000 shorter lines and hooks are attached to the long line.

Gillnetters are fairly small boats. Their gill nets are made of clear, thin line. Passing schools of fish can't see the net, so they swim blindly into it and are tangled.

Trappers include the lobster boats of Maine, New Brunswick, and Nova Scotia. These boats drop baited metal traps to the sea bottom. Later, the boats return to pull up the traps and the lobsters inside them.

Nets bulge from the stern of the Susan Rae. *The white* (left) *and tan* (right) *objects in the net float to keep the upper part of the net afloat.*

SPORTFISHING BOATS

There aren't as many kinds of sportfishing boats as there are sport fish. But sportfishing boats come in a huge number of shapes and sizes.

Sportfishing boats are usually in the 15 to 30 foot (4.6-9.1 meter) range. They may have an outboard, inboard, or inboard-outboard motor. Some of the most powerful sportfishing boats have two motors working together.

The smallest, lightest fishing boats may use an electric motor.

Twin outboard engines power this sportfishing boat. The boat has several fishing-rod holders along the deck rail and on the roof frame.

KINDS OF SPORTFISHING BOATS

A fishing boat is built for the type of water in which it will be used most often. Big boats with V-shaped **hulls** (HUHLZ) are built to handle rough water. Flat-bottom boats, like flats boats, are built for calm, shallow water.

While sportfishing boats are different, they share features. For example, they have plenty of room on their decks. That way, fishermen can move freely about to cast or fight a hooked fish.

This type of small, open, flat-bottomed boat is ideal for fishing in calm, shallow water.

In many open sportfishing boats, the controls are located in a center console. That leaves plenty of space around the deck for fishing and fishing poles.

Fishing boats have built-in fish boxes, iceboxes, live wells for bait, rod holders, and cutting boards. Flats and bass boats have a seat built above the deck at the rear, or stern, of the boat.

Many fishing boats have the latest electronic equipment for safety and finding fish.

GLOSSARY

cannery (KAN nur ree) — a factory that puts fish into sealed cans

commercial (kuh MUR shuhl) — those who do something for the purpose of making money, such as commercial fishermen

deck (DEK) — the covered area across the top of a ship or boat hull; any one of the platforms, or floors, built above the bottom of a hull

hull (HUHL) — the floating shell of a boat or ship

multipurpose (MUL tuh pur pus) — that which is used for more than one job or activity

process (PRAH sess) — to make whole fish into meat by cleaning them, cutting them up, and wrapping, canning, or freezing them

seine (SANE) — a type of fish net, usually shaped like a huge purse and set along the water surface

trawl (TROL) — a type of fish net, usually shaped like a funnel and sometimes set in water more than one-half mile (.8 kilometers) deep

vessel (VEH sul) — a boat or ship

INDEX

FURTHER READING

Find out more about fishing boats with these helpful books:
• Armentrout, David. *Fishing.* Rourke, 1998
• Butterfield, Moira. *Look Inside Cross Sections Ships.* Dorling Kindersley, 1994
• Graham, Ian. *Boats, Ships, Submarines and Other Floating Machines.* Kingfisher, 1993
• Humble, Richard. *Submarines and Ships.* Viking, 1997
• Travis, George. *Let's Go Fishing for a Living.* Rourke, 1998